Bonus Material: Bring the Bible to Life!

Watch the Bible stories come alive by downloading the FREE Augmented Reality app from B&H Kids. Then just scan the icons at the beginning of each story to hear short summary narrations by Jenna Lucado and see full-color illustrations jumping right off the page!

DOWNLOAD THE FREE APP NOW

Scan this QR code or search in the app store for "B&H Kids AR." Then it's as easy as 1, 2, 3 . . .

Tap any icon

Scan the illustration

Watch it come to life!

Illustrations by Heath McPherson

ISBN: 978-1-4336-8529-3
Dewey Decimal Classification: J220.95
Subject Heading: BIBLE STORIES \ BIBLE—HISTORY
OF BIBLICAL EVENTS \ BIBLE—PICTORIAL WORKS

Printed in Hui Zhou, Guang Dong, China,
March 2016.

2 3 4 5 6 7 • 20 19 18 17 16

BIBLE STORIES in 5 minutes

B&H KIDS
Nashville, Tennessee

Table of Contents

In the Beginning

–from Genesis 1–3

This is the story of Adam and Eve and of how God created everything from nothing.

In the beginning, there was nothing, only God. Then God created the heavens and the earth. But the earth was dark and cold. There was no sun or moon. No trees or flowers. No lions or zebras or bears. There were no people anywhere. There was only darkness.

Then God said, "Let there be light," and there was! God called the light "day" and the dark "night." That was the first day of creation.

On the second day, God created a great space above the earth. He called it "sky." On the third day, God made the land and the seas. Then God said, "Let the land be filled with plants and trees." And it was!

On the fourth day, God made the sun to light up the day. Then He scattered the stars across the sky and made the moon to give light to the night.

On the fifth day, God made every creature that swims and splashes in the seas—from starfish to whales and everything in between!

Next, God filled the skies with birds of every kind. Bright little bluebirds and soaring eagles, birds that chirp and birds that sing.

On the sixth day, God made all the animals. He made animals that hop and run, and He made creatures that creep and crawl. He made the tiniest of mice and the elephant that weighs a ton!

But there was still one more creation for God to create. So He gathered together the dust of the ground. He shaped it and formed it just right. Then God breathed the breath of life into man! And the man was called Adam.

God planted a garden in a place called Eden, and He placed Adam there. Then God brought each animal to Adam, one by one, for him to name. And whatever Adam called it, that's what the animal's name became.

But even after seeing every animal God had made, Adam couldn't find a helper or friend. No other creature was like him.

So God made Adam fall deeply asleep, and then He took a rib from Adam's side. From the rib, God made a woman. She was called Eve, and she became Adam's helper and friend. That was the end of the sixth day.

God then looked around at all He had made, and He saw that it was very good. So on the seventh day, God rested from all He had done.

Adam and Eve had only one thing they weren't allowed to do in the garden.

"You may eat fruit from any tree, any tree except one," God warned. "Don't eat fruit from the tree of the knowledge of good and evil, or you will surely die."

Now the serpent (who was really Satan) was the sneakiest of all the animals. One day, he slipped up to Eve and said, "Did God really say, 'Don't eat fruit from *any* tree'?"

"No," said Eve. "We can eat any fruit, except fruit from the tree of the knowledge of good and evil. If we eat it or even touch it, we will die!"

"You won't die," the serpent hissed. "But if you eat it, you'll be like God."

Eve looked at the fruit. It did look tasty, and she wanted to be wise like God. So she took a bite and gave some to Adam too. Suddenly, their eyes were opened, and they knew they were naked! So they snatched up some leaves to make clothes.

Then Adam and Eve heard something! It was God, walking in the garden. They were frightened because they had disobeyed God, so they hurried to hide.

"Where are you?" God called, even though He already knew.

Adam trembled and said, "I was afraid because I was naked. So I hid from You."

"Who said you were naked?" God asked. "Did you eat the fruit I told you not to eat?"

“It was the woman,” Adam exclaimed. “She gave the fruit to me!”

But Eve said, “It was the serpent. He lied to me!”

Adam and Eve had broken God's rule, so they had to leave His garden. God sent an angel and a fiery, swirling sword to stand guard so they could never again get in.

From that time on, Adam and Eve had to work very hard for their food. And one day they would die, just as God had said.

When Adam and Eve disobeyed God, sin came into the world. But God didn't stop loving them. In fact, He already had a plan to save them—and to save you and me, too!

One day, when the time was exactly right, God would send Jesus, His Son. Jesus rescues people from sin when they repent and believe in Him.

"For God loved the world in this way:
He gave His One and Only Son, so that everyone who believes in Him will not perish but have eternal life."
—John 3:16

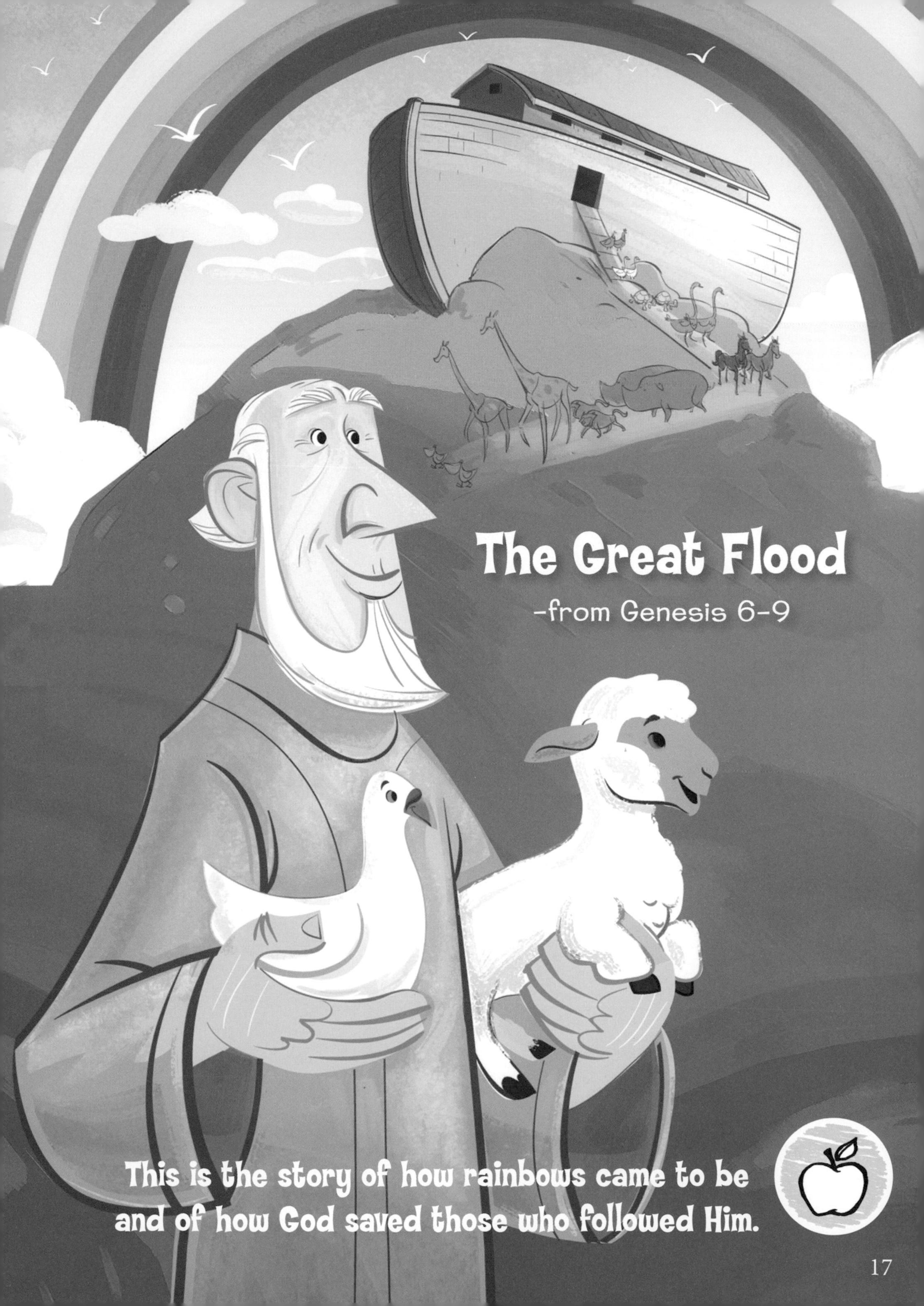

The Great Flood

-from Genesis 6-9

This is the story of how rainbows came to be and of how God saved those who followed Him.

Adam and Eve had children. And their children had children, and so on, and so on, until people filled the earth. But as the years passed, the people began to forget about God. Their hearts and minds filled up with wickedness. They became so wicked that they only thought about evil all the time!

This made God sad. It made God *so* sad that He was sorry He had ever made man. So God decided to destroy all the living creatures on the earth. But one man was different.

That man's name was Noah, and he had three sons. They were named Shem, Ham, and Japheth. Noah tried to please God in all he did and said. And that made God happy.

One day, God said to Noah, "I am going to flood the earth and destroy every creature on it. But because you love Me and follow Me, I am going to save you and your family." Then God told Noah to build an ark.

"Build it out of gopher wood," God said. "Put a roof on top and a door in the side. And when the time comes, take your family with you into the ark. Then I will send two of every animal on earth to you. Take them into the ark and keep them safe."

Noah listened to God and did everything just as He said. Noah was 600 years old when all this happened.

When the ark was finished, God sent the animals to Noah. Every kind of bird, every animal, every creeping and crawling creature. Two by two, they came to Noah.

When all the animals were inside, God said to Noah, "Go into the ark, you and all your family."

Noah did just as God said, and God shut the door. Then it began to rain.

Waters poured down from the sky. And more waters shot up from beneath the earth! For forty days and forty nights, it rained and rained and rained.

The waters grew deeper and deeper until the ark floated up off the ground. Higher and higher, the waters rose until it was everywhere—even covering the tops of the trees! Still, the waters rose higher.

Up and up and up they rose until the tops of the very tallest mountains were covered.

But Noah and all his family and all the animals were safe and warm and dry on the ark.

After forty days the rains stopped, but the earth was still flooded. So God sent a great wind to dry up the waters. The wind *whistled* and *whooshed* around the ark.

The waters sank lower and lower until, at last, the tips of the mountaintops could be seen. Then one day the ark landed with a *thump* and a *thud* on the mountains called Ararat.

Noah waited forty days. Then he opened the window of the ark and sent out a raven. The bird flew back and forth until the waters had dried up. Next Noah sent out a dove. But the dove couldn't find a place to land—not even a tree! So she hurried back to Noah in the ark.

Noah waited seven more days and sent out the dove again. This time she came back with an olive leaf held tightly in her beak. The trees were growing again! Noah waited seven more days and sent out the dove yet again. This time she did not return. The waters were gone!

God said, "Noah! Come out of the ark—you and all your family and all the animals!"

Noah and his wife, his sons, and their wives all stepped out of the ark, stretching and blinking in the bright sunshine. The animals followed, two by two. Birds fluttered their wings and soared into the sky. Lions and leopards crouched and crept. Bears lumbered along while the turtles plodded slowly out.

There was so much to see and do, but Noah stopped and worshipped God. God blessed Noah and his sons and told them to fill the earth with people again. Then God made a covenant —a very special promise—with Noah and his sons.

"Never again will I destroy the earth with a flood," promised God. And as a sign of that promise, God placed a rainbow in the clouds.

"Whenever I see the rainbow," God said, "I will remember My promise."

God punished the people of the world for their wickedness and sins. But God showed mercy and grace to Noah and his family.

There is still wickedness and sin in this world today, but God has now fully revealed His amazing plan to rescue you and me. Jesus, God's own Son, was punished for our sins so that those who love and follow Him don't have to be!

[Jesus] gave Himself for our sins to rescue us.
—Galatians 1:4

The Dreamer

-from Genesis 37, 39-50

This is the story of
a man named Joseph
and of how God used
the evil plans of some
to save the lives of many.

Long, long ago, there lived a man named Jacob who had twelve sons. But he loved his son Joseph best of all and gave him a beautiful robe of many colors. This made Joseph's brothers hate him.

Some time later, Joseph dreamed that he and his brothers were gathering bundles of grain. Suddenly Joseph's bundle stood straight up while the others all bowed down to him.

When Joseph told his brothers about the dream, they said, "Do you really think we'll bow down to you?" And they hated him even more!

One day, Jacob sent Joseph to check on his brothers, who were in the fields with their flocks. The brothers saw him coming and planned a way to kill him.

But one brother said, “Don’t kill him! Throw him into this pit instead.” So the brothers did just that.

When a caravan of Ishmaelites passed by, the brothers sold Joseph to them as a slave. They then dipped his beautiful robe in animal blood and gave it to their father. Jacob thought a wild animal had killed his son!

Meanwhile, Joseph was taken to Egypt and sold to a man named Potiphar. But God was with Joseph and blessed him in everything he did. Potiphar saw this and put him in charge of all his household.

When Potiphar's wife wanted Joseph to betray his master, Joseph said, "No!" So she told a terrible lie about him, and Potiphar threw him in prison!

But even in prison, God was with Joseph. Soon he was in charge of all the other prisoners.

Some time later, Pharaoh (the king) became angry with his cupbearer and baker and put them in prison too. There they both dreamed strange dreams. With God's help, Joseph explained their dreams: the cupbearer would go back to his job, but the baker would die.

"Tell Pharaoh about me," Joseph begged the cupbearer. But when the cupbearer returned to Pharaoh, he forgot all about Joseph.

Two years later, Pharaoh also dreamed strange dreams. Seven plump, healthy cows were eaten by seven thin, ugly cows! And seven thin heads of grain ate up seven fat heads of grain. No one could tell Pharaoh what the dreams meant. Suddenly the cupbearer remembered Joseph!

With God's help, Joseph said, "Your dreams mean there will be seven years of plenty followed by seven years of famine. You should appoint a man to gather up all the extra food during the good years. Then store it so that Egypt won't starve during the famine."

Pharaoh said, "*You* will be that man. You will be over all of Egypt. Only I will be greater than you, Joseph."

During the seven good years, Joseph stored up all the extra grain. When the famine came, only Egypt had grain. People from every nation came to Joseph to buy food.

Jacob even sent his sons to Egypt to buy grain. But the youngest son, Benjamin, didn't go. Jacob was afraid something might happen to him.

Joseph's brothers came and bowed before him. Joseph knew them instantly, but they did not know him. Joseph pretended to be angry and called them spies. Then he threw them in prison.

After three days, Joseph kept one brother in prison and sent the rest home. "Don't come back unless you bring your youngest brother with you," he said. "Then I will know you aren't spies."

The brothers told their father all that had happened. Still, Jacob wouldn't let Benjamin go. But soon the grain was gone, and Jacob had no choice. If Benjamin didn't go to Egypt, they would all starve.

So once more the brothers went to see Joseph. But after their bags were filled with grain, Joseph secretly ordered that his own silver cup be hidden in Benjamin's bag.

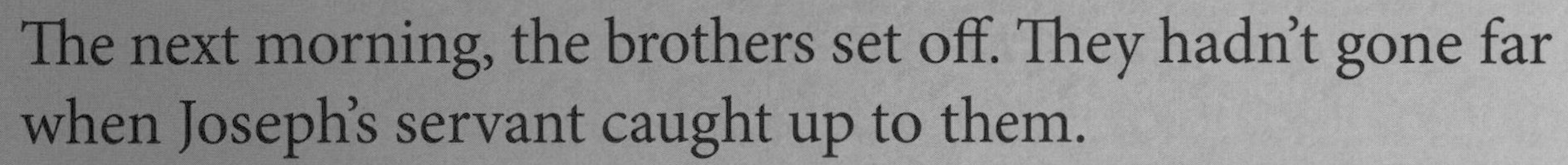
The next morning, the brothers set off. They hadn't gone far when Joseph's servant caught up to them.

"Why have you stolen my master's cup?" he said.

"We didn't steal anything!" the brothers said.

But the cup was found in Benjamin's sack! The brothers tore their clothes in sadness and returned to Joseph's house. There they fell to the ground before him.

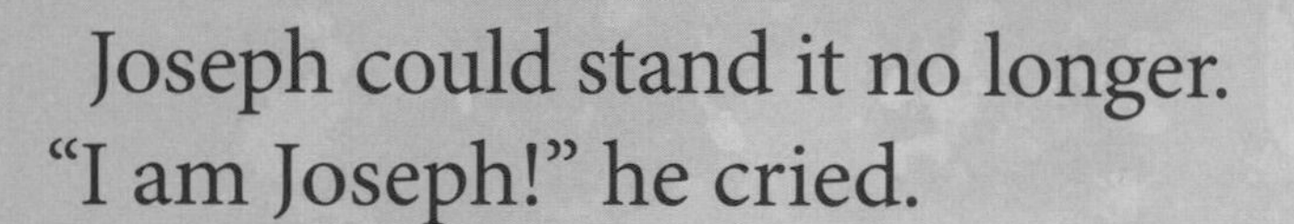

Joseph could stand it no longer. "I am Joseph!" he cried.

The brothers were terrified, but Joseph said, "Don't be worried or angry with yourselves. God sent me here ahead of you to keep you alive. Go back and bring my father and all your families here. I will make sure you have plenty of food."

Joseph's brothers did as he said, and that is how the Hebrew people came to live in Egypt.

Joseph's brothers had planned to hurt him by selling him as a slave. But God took their evil plan and used it to save not only their lives but many more lives as well.

In the same way, the men who put Jesus on the cross had an evil plan. But God used their plan for the great good of all His people.

We know that all things work together for the good of those who love God.
—Romans 8:28

Mighty Miracles

–from Exodus 1–15

This is the story of how a great sea was parted and of how God rescued His people.

Years after Joseph died, another pharaoh ruled over Egypt. He didn't know about Joseph or all that he had done for Egypt. This pharaoh saw that his land was filled with Joseph's people, the Israelites (or Hebrews). He was afraid they would help Egypt's enemies, so he made them his slaves. Then he commanded a most terrible command: every Israelite baby boy must be thrown into the Nile River!

But Jochebed just couldn't throw her baby boy into the river! For three months, she kept him a secret. When he grew too big to hide, she tucked him in a basket and nestled it into the reeds by the river. Miriam, the baby's sister, hid nearby to watch over him.

The basket was soon found by Pharaoh's own daughter! When she saw the crying baby, she felt sorry for him.

Miriam ran to her. "Should I get an Israelite woman to care for him?" she asked.

Pharaoh's daughter agreed, and Miriam hurried to get the baby's own mother! When the boy grew older, Jochebed brought him to Pharaoh's daughter. He became her son, and she named him Moses.

Years later, Moses saw an Egyptian beating an Israelite slave. He was so angry that he killed the Egyptian. But Pharaoh found out and tried to kill Moses!

Moses ran away and became a shepherd in Midian. When Pharaoh finally died, another pharaoh took his place. But life was still terrible for the Israelites. They cried out to God for help, and He heard them.

One day, Moses was out tending the sheep when he saw something strange. A bush was on fire, but it didn't burn up!

Suddenly God spoke from the bush, "Moses! I'm sending you to lead My people out of Egypt."

But Moses didn't want to go! "I'm not good at speaking," he said. "Please send someone else."

God became angry, but He said, "Aaron, your brother, will meet you. He'll speak for you."

Moses traveled back to Egypt. Together, he and Aaron went to Pharaoh and said, "Yahweh, the God of Israel, says: Let My people go."

But Pharaoh said, "Who is Yahweh, and why should I obey Him? I will not let Israel go!"

God sent Moses and Aaron down to the Nile River. "When you see Pharaoh by the river, strike the water with your staff."

When the staff struck the river, the water turned to blood! All the fish died, and the water smelled so bad that no one could drink it. Still, Pharaoh would not let God's people go.

So God made frogs swarm up out of the Nile. They hopped into the palace, into Pharaoh's bedroom, and right up onto his bed! They croaked from every oven, bowl, and pot in Egypt. But Pharaoh still would not let God's people go.

So God sent more plagues. He turned the dust of the earth into biting, stinging gnats. Then swarms of flies filled every house. Animals died, and the people were covered with painful sores. Hail beat down crops and shattered trees. Swirling clouds of locusts ate every last plant. Then three days of thick, black darkness covered all Egypt. Only the Israelites had light. Still, Pharaoh would not let God's people go.

Then God sent one last plague, the most terrible one of all. But He told Moses how to keep the Israelites safe.

"Sacrifice a sheep or a goat, and paint your doorposts with its blood," Moses said. "When God sees the blood, He'll pass over your house, and you'll be safe."

At midnight the Lord struck down every firstborn son in Egypt, from Pharaoh's son to the lowliest prisoner's son. A great cry of sadness was heard throughout Egypt.

"Go!" Pharaoh shouted at Moses and Aaron. "Take your people and your animals, and go!"

The Israelites hurried to leave Egypt. God led them toward the Red Sea, guiding them with a pillar of cloud by day and a pillar of fire by night.

But when Pharaoh saw that his slaves were gone, he changed his mind! "Bring the chariots!" he ordered. Then he and his entire army chased after the Israelites. The Israelites saw them coming and were terrified!

But Moses said, "Don't be afraid. God will fight for you!" Then he stretched out his hand over the Red Sea. God sent a powerful wind that drove the sea back, and the Israelites walked across on dry ground!

The Egyptians chased them into the sea, but God made their chariots swerve and crash. Moses stretched out his hand again, and God sent the waters rushing back. Pharaoh's entire army was swept into the sea!

God's people were saved!

God used mighty miracles to rescue His people from slavery to Egypt. Many years later, Jesus used mighty miracles to show that He truly was the Son of God and had come to rescue His people from slavery to sin.

Sin will not rule over you,
because you are not under law but under grace.
—Romans 6:14

The Boy and the Giant

–from 1 Samuel 16-17

This is the story of a young shepherd boy who faced a mighty giant and of how he trusted God to save him.

The Israelites wanted a king, so God gave them Saul. Saul was a good king, at first. But then he began to disobey God. So God decided to choose a new king.

"Go to Bethlehem," God told His prophet Samuel. "And find a man named Jesse. I've chosen one of his sons to be Israel's new king. I'll show you which one."

So Samuel traveled to Bethlehem. After seeing Jesse's oldest son, Samuel thought, *Surely he must be the new king!*

But God said, "No, it isn't him. You can only see what's on the outside of a man, but I can see inside his heart."

So Jesse brought his next son to Samuel. And his next. And his next. And his next. Seven sons paraded before Samuel. But each time, God said, "No."

“Do you have any more sons?” Samuel asked.

So Jesse sent for his youngest son, David, who was out tending sheep.

When David came, God said, “He’s the one! Anoint him.”

Samuel took a horn of oil and poured it over David. And from that day on, the Spirit of the Lord was with him.

But the Spirit of the Lord left Saul, and an evil spirit came to trouble him.

"Music will help you feel better," Saul's servants said. "Let us find someone to play the harp for you."

One servant remembered that David played the harp and sent for him. Whenever the evil spirit troubled Saul, David would play his harp, and Saul would feel better. So David traveled back and forth from watching his father's sheep to play for Saul.

Now Israel was at war with the Philistines. The Philistine army gathered on one hill while Saul and the Israelites faced them on another hill.

The Philistines had a warrior named Goliath, and he was a giant! He stood nine feet and nine inches tall. His armor weighed 125 pounds! He carried a huge bronze sword and a spear with a heavy iron point.

One day, Goliath marched out and shouted, "There's no need for all of us to fight! Choose one man to fight me. If he wins, we'll be your servants. But if I win, then you'll be our servants."

Saul and the Israelites were terrified! No one wanted to fight Goliath.

Every morning and every evening for forty days, Goliath marched out and shouted his challenge to the Israelites. But no one dared to fight him.

Jesse's three oldest sons were at the battle with Saul. One day, Jesse told David to go and check on his brothers. David reached their camp and found his brothers just as Goliath came marching out. He listened to the giant's shouts and then watched as all the Israelites trembled with fear.

"Who is this Philistine to challenge the armies of the living God?" David demanded.

King Saul heard about what David had said and sent for him.

"I'll fight this Goliath for you!" David told Saul.

"You can't fight that giant," said Saul. "You're just a boy!"

But David said, "When a lion or a bear attacks my father's sheep, I grab it by its fur and strike it down. This giant will be like one of them. God saved me from the lion and bear, and He'll save me from Goliath."

Saul agreed to let David fight and even gave him his own armor to wear. David strapped it on and tried to walk. "I can't even walk in these!" he said and took them off. Instead, David took his own staff and sling. Then, after putting five smooth stones in his pouch, he set off to face Goliath.

When Goliath saw David coming, he shouted, "Am I a dog that you come to fight me with sticks?"

But David said, "You come to fight me with a spear and a sword, but I come in the name of God. And He will hand you over to me."

David ran toward Goliath. As he ran, he slipped a stone into his sling. Round and round went the sling. At just the right moment, David let go, and the stone sailed through the air. It hit Goliath right in the forehead, and he fell face-down on the ground!

When the Philistines saw that their hero was dead, they ran away. The Israelites gave a great shout and chased after them.

And that was how God used David, a young shepherd boy, to defeat the mighty giant Goliath.

In David, we see a picture of courageous faith in God's power. We also catch a glimpse of the coming King who no one would have expected or picked to win the victory—Jesus. Because He died and rose again, He is mighty to save.

"You will have suffering in this world.
Be courageous! I have conquered the world."
—John 16:33

The Brave Queen

–from the book of Esther

This is the story of a brave queen and of how God placed her in just the right place at just the right time to save her people.

King Ahasuerus was looking for a queen. So all the beautiful young women in his kingdom were brought to his palace. Esther was one of them.

Esther was very beautiful. She was also a Jew. When she went to the palace, her uncle Mordecai warned her not to tell anyone that she was Jewish. This was because not everyone liked God's people.

Esther and all the other young women were given a whole year of beauty treatments before they even could see the king. At last, it was Esther's turn to go to the king, and he loved her best of all! So he placed a royal crown upon her head and made her his queen.

One day, Mordecai overheard two guards plotting to kill King Ahasuerus. He warned Esther, and she warned the king. The plot was stopped, and Mordecai's bravery was written in the king's book of history.

Now Haman was one of the king's officials. All the people bowed down to him—except Mordecai. Haman was furious!

He decided to destroy Mordecai and all the Jewish people too. So Haman lied to the king. "There are people who don't obey your laws," he said. "They should be destroyed."

The king didn't like people disobeying him! "Do as you see fit," he told Haman.

So Haman ordered the king's officials to destroy all the Jews —young and old—on the thirteenth day of the twelfth month.

When Mordecai heard about the order, he tore his clothes and wept bitterly. Esther sent a servant to find out what was wrong. Mordecai sent a message back to her: "Tell the queen she must go to the king and beg him to save her people."

But Esther said, "If I go to the king without being called for, I could be killed! Only if the king holds out his golden scepter will I live."

Mordecai answered, "Don't think you'll be safe just because you live in the palace! Who knows? Maybe you were made queen so that you could save your people."

So Esther sent word to Mordecai to gather all the Jews and fast for three days. "I and my servants will fast too," she said. "Then, I will go to the king. And if I die, I die."

Mordecai did just as Esther asked.

On the third day, Esther dressed in her most royal clothing. Trembling, she went to see the king. When the king saw her, he held out his golden scepter to her and said, "What is it, Queen Esther? I'll give you whatever you want, even up to half my kingdom."

"If it pleases the king," Esther said, "will you and Haman come to a banquet today?"

The king was pleased. At the banquet, he again said, "I'll give you whatever you want, even up to half my kingdom."

But Esther only said, "I ask that you and Haman come to another banquet tomorrow. Then I'll tell you what I want."

Haman left the palace full of joy that day. He'd been invited to *two* royal banquets! But on his way home he saw Mordecai and was filled with anger again. When he told his wife and friends about Mordecai, they said, "Have a gallows built. Then ask the king to hang Mordecai on it." So Haman did just that.

That night, King Ahasuerus couldn't sleep, so a servant read to him the story of how Mordecai saved his life. "What has been done to honor Mordecai?" the king asked.

"Nothing," answered his servants.

The king asked Haman, "How should the king honor a man?"

Thinking the king wanted to honor *him*, Haman said, "Dress him in the king's own robe and put him on the king's own horse. Then have the king's most noble official parade him through the city square."

This pleased the king, so he said, "Do just as you said for Mordecai."

Haman obeyed, but he did *not* like it!

At Esther's second banquet, the king once again said to her, "I'll give you whatever you want, even up to half my kingdom."

This time Esther answered. "Please save my life," she begged, "and the lives of my people!"

King Ahasuerus was shocked! "Who dares to threaten the queen?"

"Haman!" said Esther.

The king was so angry that he stormed out of the room.

Haman fell onto the couch where Esther sat, begging her to save his life. The king returned and saw Haman. "Would he hurt the queen in my own palace?" he shouted.

Then a servant said, "There's a gallows at Haman's house. He built it for Mordecai."

"Hang Haman on it!" the king ordered. So it was done.

And *that* is how brave Queen Esther saved the lives of all her people.

Queen Esther bravely spoke to the king to save her people. Jesus also speaks to the King for His people, asking Him to protect us and forgive us.

"Holy Father, protect them by
Your name that You have given Me."
—John 17:11

The Birth of a King

-from Luke 1-2 and Matthew 1-2

This is the story of God's great plan to save His people and of how it connected to a tiny baby Boy.

The angel Gabriel was one of God's special messengers. One day, God sent him to see a young woman named Mary, who lived in the town of Nazareth. Gabriel appeared suddenly before Mary and said, "Rejoice! The Lord is with you."

Mary was frightened! She'd never seen an angel before.

"Don't be afraid," Gabriel said. "God is pleased with you. You're going to have a son, and you will name Him Jesus. He will be called the Son of the Most High."

"But how can I have a son?" Mary asked. "I'm not married yet."
"The Child will be the Son of God," Gabriel told her. "Remember your relative Elizabeth? No one thought she would ever have a child, but now she's going to have a baby. That's because nothing is impossible with God!"
So Mary said, "Let everything happen just as you've said."

After the angel left, Mary just had to see Elizabeth. So she hurried to the town where Elizabeth lived. When Mary walked into her relative's house, she called out to her. At the sound of Mary's voice, Elizabeth's baby leaped with joy inside her! Mary stayed with Elizabeth for some three months before she went back home to Nazareth.

Now Mary was engaged to marry Joseph, who was from the family of King David. When Joseph discovered that Mary was going to have a baby, he was very sad. But he was a kind man and didn't want to shame her in front of everyone.

So he decided to tell her quietly that he wanted to end the engagement.

After Joseph had decided this, an angel came to him in a dream. "Take Mary as your wife," the angel told him. "The baby is from God, and you will name Him Jesus. He will save His people from their sins."

When Joseph woke up, he did exactly as the angel said: he married Mary.

Soon after, Caesar Augustus ordered everyone to return to his own town to be counted in a census. So Joseph traveled to Bethlehem, the city of David, because he was from the family of David. He took Mary with him, and they went to be counted.

While they were in Bethlehem, the time came for Mary to have her baby. Because there was no room for them anywhere else, Mary and Joseph found shelter where the animals were kept. Mary gave birth to her Son and wrapped Him snugly in cloths. Then she laid Him in a feeding trough.

Nearby, some shepherds were out in the fields, keeping watch over their flocks through the night. Suddenly, an angel of the Lord appeared to them and said, "Don't be afraid! I bring you good news for all people. Today a Savior has been born for you in the city of David. You'll find Him wrapped in cloths and lying in a feeding trough."

Then the sky filled with angels, praising God and saying: "Glory to God in heaven, and peace on earth to His people!"

The shepherds said to one another, "We must go and see this Child!" So they hurried off to Bethlehem. There they found Mary and Joseph and the Baby lying in a feeding trough, just as the angel had said.

The shepherds told Mary and Joseph all that the angels had said about the Child. Mary listened carefully and treasured their words in her heart.

Some time after this, wise men from the east came to Jerusalem. "Where is the One who has been born King of the Jews?" they asked. "We saw His star and have come to worship Him."

Now Herod was king at that time, and this news made him very upset. *I am king!* he thought. So he gathered the chief priests and scribes and asked where the Savior would be born.

"In Bethlehem," they told him.

Then Herod called for the wise men and said, "Go and search for the Child. When you find Him, tell me where He is so I can worship Him too."

So the wise men went on their way. They followed the star to the house where Jesus was. When they saw Him, they fell down and worshipped Him, and they gave Him gifts of gold, frankincense, and myrrh. Then, being warned in a dream not to go back to Herod, they went home to their own country by another way.

After the wise men left, an angel of the Lord again came to Joseph in a dream. "Get up!" said the angel. "Herod wants to destroy the Child! Take Jesus and Mary, and run away to Egypt."

So Joseph got up that very night and escaped with Mary and Jesus to Egypt. They stayed there until after King Herod died.

From the very beginning of the world, God planned to send His Son to save His people. But Jesus didn't come as a great and powerful King to rule the earth. He came as a tiny baby to rule in our hearts.

"Love the Lord your God with all your heart, with all your soul, with all your mind, and with all your strength."
—Mark 12:30

Jesus Grows Up

–from Matthew 2-4 and Luke 2-6

This is the story of how Jesus grew up and of how the Son of God began the work of saving His people.

To escape the evil King Herod, an angel told Joseph to flee to Egypt with Jesus and Mary. Years passed, and the king died. Then an angel again came to Joseph in a dream and said, "Get up! It's safe to leave Egypt now. Take Jesus and His mother and go back to Israel."

So Joseph woke up and did just that. The family settled in the town of Nazareth, in the area of Galilee, in the land of Israel. And that's where Jesus grew up.

Every year, Mary and Joseph traveled all the way to the city of Jerusalem to celebrate the Passover Festival. When Jesus was twelve years old, He went with them. After the festival, Mary and Joseph started the long journey back home. They were traveling with a large group of family and friends, and they thought Jesus was with them—but He wasn't!

A whole day passed before Mary and Joseph discovered that Jesus was missing. They ran around to all their family and friends, asking, "Have you seen Jesus?" But no one had! So they raced back to Jerusalem to look for Him there.

All through the city, Mary and Joseph searched for Jesus. They looked high and they looked low, but He was nowhere to be found! At last, after three days of searching, they found Him. Jesus was sitting in the temple, listening to the teachers and asking questions.

"Jesus!" Mary said. "Your father and I have been searching everywhere for You! Why have You treated us this way?"

But Jesus said, "Why did you search for Me? Didn't you know I had to be in My Father's house?"

Mary didn't really understand what Jesus' words meant, but she stored them in her heart to think about later. Jesus went back to Nazareth with His parents and obeyed them in all things. He grew taller and wiser, and He pleased both God and people.

Now John, who was the son of Mary's relative Elizabeth, also grew up. He went out into the wilderness to preach about the Savior who was coming. He told people that they should be baptized to show that they were truly sorry for their sins. (That's why he was called John the Baptist.)

Some people asked John if *he* was the Savior. "No!" said John. "I only baptize you with water, but He will baptize you with the Holy Spirit. I'm not even good enough to untie His sandals."

Then, one day, Jesus asked John to baptize Him. But John said, "No! You should baptize me!"

"This is the way it has to be," Jesus told him.

So John baptized Jesus in the Jordan River. As Jesus came up out of the water, the heavens opened up, and the Spirit of God came down on Him like a dove. Then the voice of God spoke from heaven and said, "This is My beloved Son!"

The Holy Spirit came and led Jesus into the wilderness. For forty days and forty nights, Jesus ate nothing at all. After that, He was very hungry! Then the Devil came to tempt Him, saying, "If You're really the Son of God, turn these stones to bread."

But Jesus said, "It is written: Man must not live on bread alone but on every word that comes from God."

Next, the Devil took Jesus to the city of Jerusalem. They stood on the very tiptop of the temple, and the Devil said, "If You're really the Son of God, throw Yourself off this temple. For it is written: His angels will not even let your foot strike against a stone."

But Jesus said, "It is also written: Do not test the Lord your God."

The Devil then took Jesus to the top of a very high mountain and showed Him all the kingdoms of the world and their riches. "I'll give You all these things," the Devil said, "if You'll worship me."

But Jesus said, "Go away, Satan! For it is written: Worship the Lord your God, and serve only Him!"

Then the Devil left Him, and angels came and served Him.

Jesus went back to Galilee and began teaching the people about God. He was filled with the power of the Holy Spirit, and everyone was amazed by His words.

When it was time to choose His disciples, Jesus went up on a mountain by Himself. All night long, He prayed to God. The next morning, Jesus chose twelve men to be His disciples. They were Peter, Andrew, James, John, Philip, Bartholomew, Matthew, Thomas, James the son of Alphaeus, Thaddeus, Simon, and Judas—the one who would betray Him.

Jesus came to earth as a baby and grew up—just like you. He bumped His head and skinned His knees—just like you. And when Jesus was tempted to do wrong, He used God's Word to defeat the Devil! He did for us what we can't do—keep God's commandments perfectly.

Jesus told him, "Go away, Satan! For it is written: Worship the Lord your God, and serve only him."
—Matthew 4:10

Jesus Teaches the People

–from Matthew 5-7

This is the story of some of Jesus' greatest teachings and of how those teachings can still change people's lives today.

Crowds of people gathered to hear Jesus. They had heard about Him and all the miracles He had done, and they wanted to see and hear Him for themselves. When Jesus saw the crowds, He went up on a mountain, sat down, and began to teach them.

He surprised the people by saying the humble and gentle people of the world are blessed by God. Those who are merciful, pure in heart, and poor in spirit are blessed.

But Jesus also warned them that some people would say bad things about them and would even be mean to them because they believed in God. "But you'll be blessed because of that," Jesus said, "and your reward in heaven will be great!"

"You are the salt of the earth," Jesus taught, "and the light of the world. No one lights a lamp and then hides it under a basket where no one can see it shine. No! The lamp is put up on a stand so that its light will fill the house.

In the same way, the good things that you do should shine in the world like a bright light. They should show everyone the goodness of God in heaven."

"Some people say that you should love your neighbor and hate your enemies," Jesus said. "But I say, love your enemies and pray for those who do wrong to you. That's what the children of God do.

“After all, if you only love those who love you back, how are you being a child of God? And if you only talk to those who talk to you, how are you different than anyone else? Anyone can do that! I want you to love your neighbors *and* your enemies too.”

Jesus also taught the people about the right way to give: "You must be careful how you give," He warned. "Don't give to the poor just to show off in front of others. Some people even sound the trumpets when they give, so that everyone will cheer for them. Don't be like them!

They already have their reward from the people, so they won't get a reward from God.

"When you give to the poor, don't let anyone see you. God will still see you, and He will reward you."

"And be careful how you pray," Jesus said. "Some people love to pray standing up where everyone can see them. Don't pray just so that others will see you. Go into a quiet room, close the door, and pray in secret. God will hear you, and He'll reward you. And don't just say a lot of words, over and over again. God knows what you need, even before you ask Him! So pray like this:

Our Father in heaven,
Your name be honored as holy.
Your kingdom come.
Your will be done
on earth as it is in heaven.
Give us today our daily bread.
And forgive us our debts,
as we also have forgiven our debtors.
And do not bring us into temptation,
but deliver us from the evil one.
For Yours is the kingdom and the power
and the glory forever. Amen.

“Don’t worry about getting lots of treasures here on earth,” Jesus said. “Those treasures can be stolen by thieves or eaten up by moths or rust. Collect treasures in heaven by doing what God says. Those treasures can *never* be stolen or destroyed!

"And don't worry about what you'll eat or drink or wear," said Jesus. "Just look at the birds: they don't plant food, but God feeds them. And look at the flowers: not even King Solomon was dressed as beautifully as the flowers. And you're worth much more than birds or flowers!

"If you will obey God and put Him first in your life, He will take care of you," Jesus promised.

Then Jesus taught the people about two kinds of builders: "Everyone who obeys My words is like the wise man who built his house on the rock. The rains poured down, and the waters rose all around. The wind roared and howled and beat against his house. But his house did not fall because it was built on the rock.

"But everyone who doesn't obey My words," Jesus warned, "will be like the foolish man who built his house on the sand. The rains poured down, and the waters rose all around. The winds roared and howled and beat against his house—and it came crashing down!"

Jesus taught the people many things that day, and they were amazed by His words.

Jesus didn't teach like ordinary teachers; He taught with the power of God! And He didn't teach ordinary lessons. Jesus taught that true righteousness comes from the inside. None of us are righteous on the inside. We are sinners, but when we trust in Jesus and the perfect life *He* lived, God changes us from the inside out.

"I am the way, the truth, and the life.
No one comes to the Father except through Me."
—John 14:6

Two Miracles

–from Matthew 14; Mark 6; Luke 9; John 6

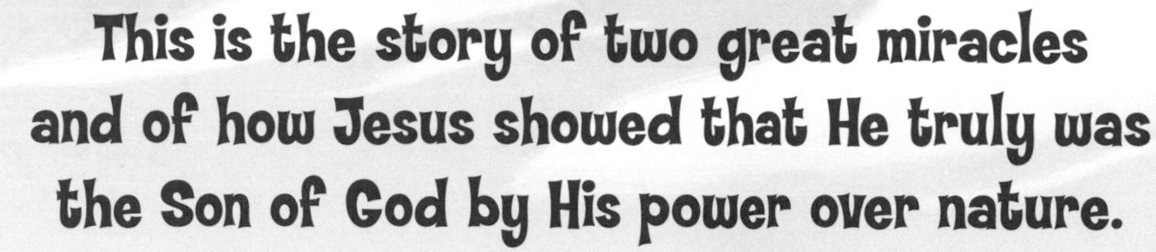

This is the story of two great miracles and of how Jesus showed that He truly was the Son of God by His power over nature.

Jesus sent His disciples out to teach the people about the coming of God's kingdom. When they returned, they wanted to tell Him all about everything they had seen and heard and done. But people were coming and going all around them. The disciples didn't even have time to eat! Jesus saw how very tired and hungry they were, so He said, "Let's go away by ourselves so you can rest."

They were near the Sea of Galilee, so they all got into a boat and sailed toward the other side. But the crowds of people saw where they were going. They ran along the shore so that they reached the other side—even before Jesus and His disciples!

Jesus stepped out of the boat and saw all the people. His heart hurt for them because they were like sheep without a shepherd. So He began to heal their sick and to teach them.

Now the place where Jesus was teaching was out in the country, away from the towns. So when evening came, the disciples went to Jesus and said, "This place is a wilderness, and it's already late. Send the people away so they can go into the villages and buy food for themselves."

"They don't need to go away," Jesus said. "You give them something to eat."

But Philip, one of the twelve disciples said, "It would take more than a year's pay to buy even a little bit of bread for this many people!" (For there were about 5,000 men gathered there, plus all the women and children.)

So Jesus said, "How many loaves do you have? Go and see."

After searching, one of His disciples named Andrew (who was Peter's brother) said, "There's a boy here who has five small loaves and two fish. But how can we feed so many people with so little food?"

Jesus simply said, "Bring them here to Me."

Now there was plenty of grass in that place, so Jesus said to the disciples, "Have the people sit down in groups of about fifty."

The people sat down and waited to see what would happen. Jesus took the five loaves and the two fish. Then, looking up to heaven, He gave thanks for them. He broke the loaves and gave them to the disciples, and the disciples gave them to the crowds. Jesus also divided the fish among all the people.

Everyone ate as much as they wanted. And the disciples still picked up twelve baskets full of leftover pieces—all from five small loaves and two little fish!

After this, Jesus told the disciples to get back in the boat. He wanted them to sail on ahead of Him to the other side while He said good-bye to the crowds of people.

After the people left, Jesus went up on the mountain by Himself to pray. When evening came, He was there alone. The disciples' boat was already out in the middle of the sea. The wind had begun to blow, and the sea was churning. The wind and the waves battered against the disciples' boat.

Around three in the morning, Jesus came walking out toward His disciples in the boat. He was walking on water! When the disciples saw Him, they were terrified. "It's a ghost!" they cried out in fear.

But Jesus called out to them, "Have courage! It is I. Don't be afraid."

Could it really be Jesus? the disciples wondered.

"Lord, if it's really You," Peter called out, "tell me to come to You on the water."

"Come!" Jesus said.

So Peter carefully climbed out of the boat. He set first one foot and then the other on top of the water. Then Peter was walking on the water too! But when he looked around him, he saw the wind and waves. He was afraid, and he began to sink. Terrified, Peter cried out, "Lord, save me!"

Immediately Jesus reached out His hand and pulled Peter up. "Why did you doubt?" Jesus asked him.

Jesus and Peter stepped into the boat. As soon as they did, the wind stopped its howling and the sea became calm. The disciples all worshipped Jesus and said, "Truly You are the Son of God!"

Jesus was no ordinary man. He was—and is—the Son of God! He was with God before the earth was created, and as the Son of God, Jesus has power over all creation. And the good news is that the One who controls creation is the same One who loves you and me!

[Jesus] was with God in the beginning.
All things were created through Him, and apart from Him
not one thing was created that has been created.
—John 1:2–3

Finding the Lost

–from Luke 15

Each of these three stories tells about how one who was lost was found again and of how God searches for those who wander away.

Jesus came to teach all people about the kingdom of God—*especially* those who were sinners. But not everyone was happy about this—*especially* the Pharisees and scribes.

One day, the Pharisees and the scribes were grumbling about Jesus. "He talks to sinners!" they exclaimed. "And He even eats with them!"

So Jesus told them this parable (a story with a special meaning):

"If a man has one hundred sheep and loses one, what does he do? He leaves the ninety-nine to search for the lost one. When he finds it, he puts it on his shoulders and happily carries it home. Then he calls out to all his friends and neighbors, 'Come and celebrate with me! I've found my lost sheep!'

"It's the same way in heaven," said Jesus. "There is more joy over one sinner who turns back to God than over the ninety-nine who didn't turn away from Him."

Then Jesus asked, “If a woman has ten silver coins and loses one of them, what does she do? She lights a lamp, sweeps out the whole house, and searches everywhere until she finds it. And when she does find it, she calls all her friends and neighbors together and says, ‘Be happy for me! I’ve found my lost coin!’

“In the same way,” Jesus said to the Pharisees and scribes, “the angels in heaven celebrate over one sinner who turns back to God.”

Jesus then told them this parable about a father and his two sons:

"A man had two sons. One day, the younger son said to his father, 'Father, give me my share of your fortune now.' This made the father very sad, but he gave the son his share of the family's fortune.

"Just a few days later, the younger son gathered up all his belongings and left. He traveled to a faraway country, where he wasted all his money on foolish living.

"After the younger son had spent all his money, a terrible famine stuck that land. He had no money and no food and no friends. He had to go to work in the fields feeding pigs. He was *so* hungry that he longed to eat the pigs' food, but no one would even give him any of that!

"One day, the son said to himself, 'I am dying of hunger, but even my father's servants have more than enough food to eat! I'll go back to my father and say to him, "Father, I have sinned against you and against heaven. I'm not worthy to be called your son. Just let me be like one of your servants."'

"Then the son got up and began the long journey back home to his father.

"While the son was still a long way off, his father saw him coming, and his heart was filled with love and compassion. The father ran to him, threw his arms around his neck, and kissed him.

"'Father,' the son said, 'I have sinned against you and against heaven. I'm not even worthy to be called your son.'

"But his father called to his servants and said, 'Quick! Bring out the best robe, and put it on my son. Bring a ring for his finger and sandals for his feet. Then kill the fattened calf, and let's have a great feast to celebrate! My son was lost to me, but now he is found again!' And so they began to celebrate.

"Now the older son had been out in the fields. When he came home, he heard all the music and dancing. 'What's going on?' he asked one of the servants.

"'Your younger brother has come home!' the servant told him. 'And your father is having a great feast to celebrate because he has his son back, safe and sound.'

"But the older brother wasn't happy—he was angry! And he refused to go into the feast. His father came out and

pleaded with him to come in. But the brother said, 'I have worked for you for years. I've done everything you've ever asked, but you never gave me even a young goat to have a small feast with my friends. But when this son who took your money and left comes home, you have a great feast for him!'

"'My son,' the father said, 'everything I have is yours. But I had to celebrate. Your brother was lost to me, but now he is found!'"

Jesus didn't come to save only the good people or the people who already know about God. He came to save all who turn from sin and trust in Him. Even when we were still sinners, He died for you and me. Now He calls us to trust Him as Savior and obey Him as Lord.

"The Son of Man has come to seek and to save the lost."
—Luke 19:10

Jesus Saves His People

–from Matthew 21-28; Mark 11-16; Luke 19-24; John 12-20; Acts 1

This is the story of Jesus' last days on earth and of how the Son of God rescued His people from sin.

Jesus and His disciples traveled toward Jerusalem for the last time. Jesus had done many wonderful and amazing things, but the chief priests and scribes were very angry with Him—so angry that they wanted to kill Him.

Jesus stopped at a small village along the way and said to two of His disciples, "Go into the village. You'll find a young donkey tied there that no one has ever ridden. Bring it here. If anyone asks what you're doing, say that the Lord needs it."

The disciples found the donkey. As they untied it, some people asked what they were doing. "The Lord needs it," they said, and the people let them go.

Jesus rode the donkey into Jerusalem. A great crowd of people came out to see Him. They covered the road with their robes and with leafy branches, and they shouted: "*Hosanna!* He who comes in the name of the Lord is the blessed One!"

When the time for Passover came, Jesus shared the meal with His twelve disciples. He took some bread, gave thanks for it, and gave it to them. "Take this," He said. "This is My body which I give for you." Then He took a cup, gave thanks, and gave it to them. "This is My blood," He said. "It is shed for the forgiveness of sins."

Then, after singing some psalms, Jesus and the disciples went out. All except Judas, the one who would betray Jesus. He had already slipped away.

Jesus and His disciples went to a garden called Gethsemane. "Wait here," Jesus said. Then He took Peter, James, and John deeper into the garden. "Stay awake with Me while I pray," He said. Then, after going a little farther, Jesus fell to the ground and prayed, "Father! If it's possible, let this cup pass from Me. But let Your will be done, not mine."

When Jesus came back, He found the disciples sleeping. "Couldn't you stay awake with Me one hour?" He asked. Jesus went away to pray again. And again, He returned to find His disciples sleeping. After praying a third time, He came back and said, "Are you still sleeping? Get up! My betrayer is coming."

At that moment, Judas appeared with a large mob of people. They were carrying swords and clubs. Judas went right up to Jesus and kissed Him—this was a sign to the mob to arrest Him. When they grabbed Jesus, all of His disciples ran away, leaving Him alone with the mob.

Jesus was taken to see the high priest.

"Tell us if You are the Son of God!" he shouted.

"You have said it," Jesus answered.

The high priest tore his robes, and the crowds shouted, "He should die!" Then they slapped Him and beat Him and spit in His face.

When morning came, they took Jesus to Pilate, the Roman governor. Pilate wanted to free Jesus, but the crowds shouted "Crucify Him!" Because Pilate was afraid of the people, he sent Jesus to be killed.

Roman soldiers twisted together a crown of thorns and put it on His head. "Hail, King of the Jews!" they laughed. Then they led Him away.

Jesus was taken to a place called Golgotha and nailed to a cross. Two criminals were crucified with Him, one on the right and one on the left. For three hours, darkness covered the land.

Then Jesus cried out, “My God, My God, why have You forsaken Me?” After that, He gave up His spirit and died. A great earthquake shook the land, and the soldiers guarding Jesus said, “He really was God’s Son!”

That evening, a follower of Jesus named Joseph of Arimathea came and asked Pilate for Jesus' body. He wrapped it in fine linen and placed it in a new tomb. After rolling a great stone in front of the tomb, he left. Pilate sent guards to watch over the tomb.

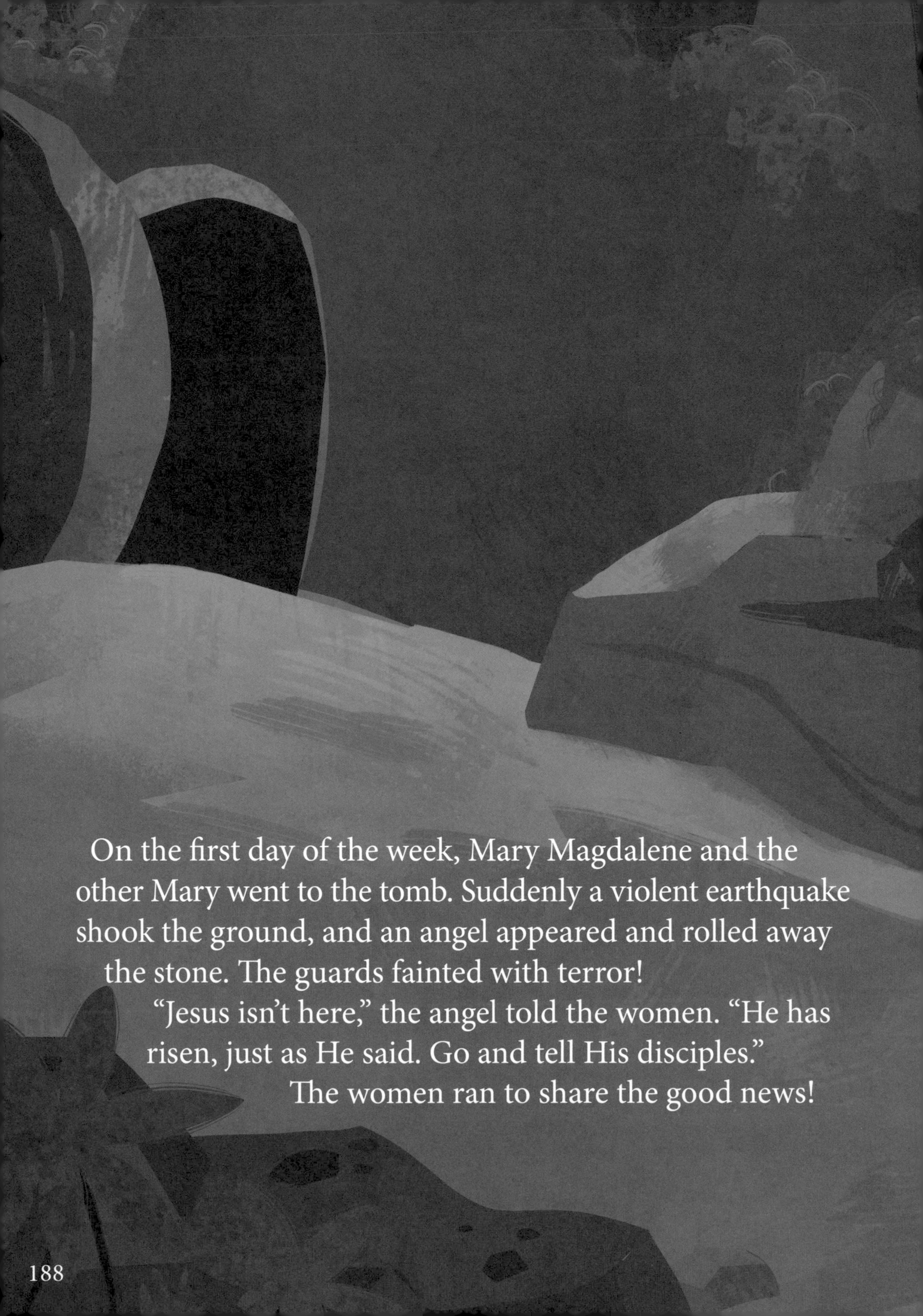

On the first day of the week, Mary Magdalene and the other Mary went to the tomb. Suddenly a violent earthquake shook the ground, and an angel appeared and rolled away the stone. The guards fainted with terror!

"Jesus isn't here," the angel told the women. "He has risen, just as He said. Go and tell His disciples."

The women ran to share the good news!

Just then Jesus stepped out to meet them. The women fell down and worshipped Him. "Don't be afraid," He said. "Go and tell the disciples to meet Me in Galilee."

Jesus stayed on the earth for another forty days and was seen by many people. Then He returned to heaven.

Before Jesus returned to heaven, He gave His disciples a job to do: go and share the Good News of His kingdom with the whole world. And Jesus gives the very same job to you—go and tell everyone all about Him!

"Go, therefore, and make disciples of all nations, baptizing them in the name of the Father and of the Son and of the Holy Spirit, teaching them to observe everything I have commanded you."
—Matthew 28:19–20

Remember:

I will praise the LORD at all times; His praise will always be on my lips.
–Psalm 34:1

Read:

Time. Everyone has it, but do we use it wisely? In Deuteronomy 6:5, God reveals how He wants us to use our time. It is the greatest of all His commandments: "Love the LORD your God with all your heart, with all your soul, and with all your strength." Every moment, from morning to night, is an opportunity to love and glorify God. Verses 6–7 explain that we can do that by keeping God's words in our heart, by talking about them wherever we go, and by obeying them in all that we do. God doesn't want to be just one *part* of our life—He wants our *whole* life to be lived through Him.

Think:

1. In the beginning God created the world and everything in it. He also created a plan to do what for His people?
2. Which of the Old Testament heroes is your favorite, and why?
3. How did that person trust in God?
4. What do all the stories of the Old Testament and New Testament have in common?
5. Jesus came to earth to save His people. Why do you think He came as a tiny baby, rather than as a mighty King?
6. The heroes of the Bible often had to be brave for God. What are some ways you can be brave enough to tell others about Him?
7. If you've got five minutes, what can you do for Jesus?

Great things start with little things. You can do great things for Jesus just by honoring Him in all the little things of your day.

For more Parent Connection ideas and activities,
visit us at BHKidsBuzz.com.

The Big Picture Interactive Bible

Available in different cover options

Ages 8-12

This full-text HCSB Bible features colorful, fully designed pages that include call-out sections. Plus a free downloadable app brings the dazzling images to life and provides narration, meeting kids in the visual world they are so accustomed to today.

The Big Picture Interactive Bible Storybook

Ages 6-10

This innovative interactive Bible storybook gives kids the big picture of God's story. It includes 145 stories with four-color illustrations, a "Christ Connection" feature showing kids how God's plan for salvation through Jesus appears throughout the Bible, and a free Augmented Reality app that brings the art and story remarkably to life both visually and audibly.

The Big Picture of What God Has Always Wanted

Ages 4-8

More than a children's book, *The Big Picture of What God Has Always Wanted* is for parents who care deeply about passing on a legacy of faith in Christ to the next generation.

The Big Picture Interactive Bible Stories for Toddlers

Ages 0-4

Introduce early learners to the Bible with these fun and engaging new storybooks designed just for toddlers. Each story features enhanced full-color illustrations that—used in conjunction with the B&H Kids Augmented Reality app—brings the pictures to life with pop-up imaging and read-a-long narration from Jenna Lucado.